Adele,

lyrics

By: ALI FARID

Title: Adele
Author: Ali Farid
Cover Design: Ali Khiabanian
ISBN: 978 1942912323
Publisher: Supreme Art, Reseda, CA, USA
LCCN (Library of Congress Control Number): 2017919037

Prepare for Publishing by **FastPublication**.com

3

To
ADELE
&
Art lovers

I would like to acknowledge my wife "FARIDEH" &
my lovely sisters
For their support, in life road

Sometimes,
I kiss her lips and she wineglass's lips
She was drunk for wine
From her, I
"MOLANA JALALEDDIN BALKHI"

1- Simple

Everything can begin straight arrow
Something;
Excuse me, what time is it?
One look and saying hello

Everything can be a complex simple
The constant restlessness

If it get start simple
Hang on, it is easy

Simples are immortal
Most love in normal

Time the simple swain
Not even asking every passer, hours
Take your phone
And to salvo hours, kiss you remote
And say I love you, inside and loud

Sometimes for everything simple is better
A tea and cake
A two person party

Two bus ticket
Easy, simplicity, more beauty

"I understand you"
Bare words
Simple sit in your heart
Bare, make you calm

Be careful guys
Remember every day
With all his wacky
You want (him)

In all his being late
You will wait
Be care full girl
If you see he is amazed
Along the days
Take him in your arms
Say softly in her eyes:
I can keep you up
Man story, care full;
Remember every time
Love you lady warm
This is that she wants

Show that your embrace
It is for her safe
To time for confusion and tears

Take her hands

Deep look in her eyes
And man say with loud and strong voice
I make love

Are you in game?
I am among in square, stand
Dance, dance, dance
So I will dance, turn around
To get drunk

Between ourselves
Your feel
So, stand out revelation in me

No wine
Even water makes me laugh
I take your hand,
You tell me:
Play enough, go home, maybe?

2- That sweet expect

Those days that your baby,
Squeezed on your chest,
You said:
"Someday, all of the people of this city,
Your name called "Our Artist"
Because your quite good sense, your melody,
Leaf to leaf, calling at hearts diary"

That belief, that sure
That sweet expectation, that loves
Now, full of flower, it is the fruitful

Not only in the whole of our town,
But around the world,
People are desirous of your child
Flowers fly
Bathed in "hurray" clamor the hall
Come and see mam!

Despite for many years,
Long hand of death,
Deposited your body to the wilderness
But your soul,
Anywhere I Sing

Like a butterfly, each side
It flies
-On me- since of the beautiful childhood age,
Smiles

Your sweet smile, donates flower,
Along with two teary eyes
Sense of pride,
Thank you mum,
Thank you

3- JACK MA

Jack: Hello "KFC", how are you?
Can you hire me?
Boss: Why should we hire you?
No, thank you

Here, the story starts

Never give up
Today is hard
Later,
Will be harder
But the end, you see sunshine

If you never give up,
Still, have a chance!
Are you small?
Focus on your mighty brain,
No physical strength

We are a good team
We know, we want to get the aim
One of us VS ten of them; we win

It doesn't matter that I lost
We found at least … the global thinks
Even I no win,
The way will open for others

Let's do this, as we are young
No time, time will no change one's mind
Wake up with the sunrise, I've motivation
Formal hours is nonsense, yea
Intellectual stimulation

Work, it can be a dream for us
As we think to the people, smart
Campaign with them to learn,
They are our live
What a wonderful thinks in mind freak
Although like the girl's arm is week,
My arms, it is okay

You need to me,
Absolutely
You need re-education to salvation
Diverse look is the other side
Of "silly thought"

Let's go to find it and must have do
With love, enjoy, Passion
Yea, it is our Mission

4-The first letter of ROMANCE is "R"

Imagine beautifully about something that they (R) not

Sit beside me, thinks:
Beautiful days,
In that future
You open letter, full of funny

Hold me tight seeing movie

One dreamy morning, next to me wear a sucks
No telling what happened last night!
Morning and long yawning
Temptation corner of my lips,
Thirsty kiss!

One chairs in the bus, together
Two hands locked,
Four explorer eyes
Hear what I say:

First letter of romance: "R"
You will stick in my heart
As delicious cheeseburger
Son, I am head over heels in love

Say something after days of uncertainty

Just,
Put your hand up my skirt
In ours first day behind a closed
I'm crying and the tired man
My sweet hand on your hand, think
Thinking beautiful on something that they(R)

5- Sparrow shouting

Twisty, your perfume in my depths moments

Extremely your picture in Purity Cup, shine
How green your dignity is in vita
Windows is still, light
You look at the garden of a long porch
Trees, grass, geranium
To sweet smile,

In kindly looking,
With eyes full of sunshine, laughing

All sparrows
In absence you
Rebuke me, like a gale
And,
Shout you by a name
Yet your shadow above dome of the pain
Inside garden, Riverside
Looking to the sheer water
Like a mirror

You are not here to see, how involve
Your poem resonates, in my song
You are not here to see, how revolve
Your soul Breeze in my garden no buds

Some midnight with cloud patches…
In canvas sky
Painted you…
Too beauty, that I want

How midnight in Playful clouds…
Boast at any moment the thousand's phase
Work like a charm magic
Know you, between all the Face
Like sleeping, just like a dream…
You are not here to see…
How I spoke about you with Wall
Rummy, answers to me, close to fall

My Star is sick with tired eyes, oh …
Rise …
In my cottage

6- Seafood restaurant

People passing by the Aquarium,
Nobody can hear me

Look at me, really in deepest
Wet between algae, my nerves
A slice no continuing of a dream, isn't likeness?

Give your hand to me, slow
See me, in front of you,
 No red,
No blue,
 Yeah, yellow

Choose from menu a dream, you don't have to settle
So, we can go in a better Eden

In your eyes,
I feel the warmth
Shake's my world,
I have fortune on my side

I would like fall across the glass,
Caught in your hands
I want to say something in your flesh,
Short talk;
Deliver me so the rest is history

Laugh a little to this fish visionary
Be sincere and tell me: MARY

7- Sad dancer girl

Pub is boiling so Excite, too hard
I'm not a temblor, Ballerina come
With golden hair and hedge skirt
Roar of joy rise drunken hearts

Music melodies take shape of cup shake
Laughter and shouts mix in space
Maze soft body, full of wave
Fire sparked in this passion way

Quake throw on body drunken, enjoy
Nude paint, my chest like ivory
Gold confetti on my clothes
Morning sun and diamond pond

My waist like a hungry snake, twisted
Smooth and slippery, like silver river
Cheater thigh,
Under reflective placket, bright
Like wrestle night as dawn moonlight

Dance ended and wino
Encouraged and tore clothes

Poured flowers to my head
Tipsy and drunk, they settled

I, but as the night before
Not happy, no flirting, no comfort

With clenched fist and inside so sad
I don't like the happiness of boastful fans
Troubled with hangovers and fever I have been
My drunk smells bitter pain and grief
Wine makes me hot and rich, oh
Yearning my life, joyfulness that I need

I give happiness to other, all my life
But my heart isn't pounding joy
Spending lifetime to give pleasure wine
I, but unfortunately can't drink, alas

Since my cry no cause sad
Sewed lips and I've burned in relax!

Like a candle, with regret fire
In dancing for people, burn higher

Oh that from the unjust Creatures night
Take the right of my tired heart

Maybe after this, from these ruins so bleak
Wish free Chains to my feet

I howl, oh cruel
My back, under the pain broke
I'm Thirsty for your blood

Do not throw flowers and kisses also

One says to me from the crowd: she is drunk
Her drunkenness tonight, lose count

Oh Look, his face black with rage
Drunk ... not! Poor is insane

Among drunkards Council, my talk
Spread strange silent and dumb
Their feedback to those drunk
After deep silence, laugh a lot!

8- **Our sequel**

You're, you are, in God, from the window of moon,
Look to me kindly and wink
You who are your face as fresh rose
Through fountains of moonlight which is my smooch
zone

You're, you are, in God, this is you in the midnight
Call me at to the moon with Love wings
You're, you're the one call me to the sky
 With name, sometime by eyes

You're, you're, I do solemnly swear, it is no longer a
dream
Dreams cannot be so bright and green
You come in my bed
To not kill me my pain

You're, you're, in god, this is the heat of your lips
On my teary eyes and afire cheeks
Sometimes in my anxiety chest, your head
Sometimes in your inflammation chest, my pate
On fire of my heart with your kind die away

I am with a dress of breeze

Open my arms to bring... you

I'm the dawn star which your eyes,
Till lull, I don't turn off

I am, I am that in all the night,
With fear and hope,
 Step into the roof of your palace
If my heart dies, not sad
Meanwhile, just have to see the sweetheart

This is not your shadow
Look flower, I'm with you
Like that fiction bird, call, flying to love,
 Until the moon goes my song

I am who that mountain chest,
Tired of my moan
From him whatever you ask,
Responds;
"I testify of the moaning in his night"

I and you get in burning in passion
Me and you are waiting for tomorrow
After the dawn come tomorrow,
What a sun!
No space between us, we are one!

9- Oh STARS!

Oh "STARS "from a far distant worlds
Your eyes are fixed upon our lightless eyes
Have you ever heard about the earth or mankind?
Within the blue sky
Haven't you seen smoke, blood, guns?

The lost land of horror in the space
The home of darkness that our nest
His intentions, your death!

Keep away from the shuttle traveling to you
Keep away from the man who step in your moon
Keep away from the man
If the man steps in your place
Your fate will be ruins as our fate

Oh stars …
You can't believe!
In my land
Wherever you go, whoever you meet
He has a dagger hidden in his fist
With each bloom of smile
Poisonous thorns has been hide

He who claims to be your join
Has nothing in mind but to loot you

If you see a blazing light in your road
It is eyes of the lupine wolf

Oh stars,
Our greeting is only a plea
Our loving is a usual lie
In the earth,
Tongue of truth has been cut

Our art:
Truth, only will be answered by whip
Whatever speaks purely to you is;
 The nightly loud weep

Oh stars, you can't believe
That the graceful pure dawn,
Blowing in the infinite space,
Fled from the earth
These dawns aren't white
The hue of earth is dark

Oh stars…
Why god doesn't pay attention to us?
The sound of our cry reaches to the welkin
Why no voice comes from the god?

10- Mystery

Who are you like?
From a strange way, Brought by the Space Storm
Oh airy fairy, you must radiate from light land
Smell essence, in your ghost
As the marvel in space, wraps

Is the flower bud in the rituals Paradise?
No one, you are a Garden daisy
By so many of elegancy,
Like the prophets by inward relevancy

Like a pearls
Your spaceship as cup of seashells
Like a red wine in shine
Like a rainbow along crystal prism
In the venus garden, on the endless heaven
Such as sunbow, your colors body is seven!!!
As the eyeful Swan at the heart of the light lake
Walk in gracefully
With all this amazing beautifully

Who are you like?
Teach me fly, to you…
Alone star that sits in aurora ruby

Star eyes, Likes what?

Like a vast plain are warm
With Clear Springs, Cool and fine

How strange your hair…
How strange your hair…
Or …Like the leaf of a willow tree, Might?
In the fountain light

You are diamond flower
Just mirror sense and your body secrets
Just your mirror knows how are you like's?

11- Prison & freedom

You … my cherry
Hi, my most wonderful audience
But you are strange, certainly!
More marry than holy marry
Praised for pure, great and noble

You're sprit of growing; the magic of green sprouts
In the sad prison fall
Bring hundreds spring

You are the most beauty of the fate laugh
A belief in the God promise
The most beauty corners of paradise

In fear plain and merciless desert
Of thirst, fatigue was forget
When dirt and blood in my life
No dead, no alive
You will fall,
As the spring water, wash it all

When all the way closed to the chess king
Sad, tired, checkmate
Hopeless, no wait
At once, blazer calls freedom, he says

But, I know, it's a big lie
You're the real, when saying freedom

With wishing you, forever
I am free tonight, it is your word!

Happy time of my world
In sobriety and sot,
Your remember is my sweetest wont
Wonder! With all this heartache
My heart beats light-hearted
Oh burning pure flame of all
The prison and freedom for I

12- My body is my business!!!

Give me the rouge, time for clarification!
To coloring my discoloration
Give me the lotion to refresh,
Faded face on my depression

Give me the perfume for aromatic,
Hairs,
And, put on my shoulders
Give me the tights dress,
As the males,
To tightly me in his embrace

Give it the naked lace
In that wrap's, get a double effect
Look at that,
Sensual and rebelling, in my face &breast

This is the cup that I drunk
So, at my misfortune, I laugh
Upon this unhappy sad face
Happy face and glamorous make

I am the prophet of the fun
For enjoy time, sing my song
Slowly in my heart,
But do you know?

No for happiness, only to survive!

What a feast, heated with me
"Peeping tom "market
Flashes on me that police officer
Sight my thigh, you! Christian father
Wow, my partner last night
What was exhausting and junks
Get ready to celebrate and then,
Called him to the scene
As the beauty deer with black eye,
I sat near the old bear
Told me: who am I like?
 I asked:
Oh I don't see look like you, "over the gold"

Other night and other mate
He was who make me sick
What if the hundred $, he paid
Its pain much more bitter, over the gain

Full of peeps but alone! No devotion
How they are boasting to the great comfort
This isn't unless for times too short

No wife, no harmonious, no heat
To cute me in love, on my head
Not my beloved child,
To out of my mind the sadness alarm

Oh! Somebody has knocking

Tonight's my wife is coming!
Oh my heart, let lose sorrow
This time, he is going to enjoy

Lips, My deceit sale lips!
Set mystery curtains on my teen
To get a few more dollars
Laugh now, Coquetry, more kiss!!!

13- Moonlight must go on vacation

"No need to light
Yeah, no need to light"

Where are you to warm my life?
Life without you is prison
Where are you my evening lights?
Run to the last gasp, I'm wiped

My lips looking for your lips
My caught smells yours
Wherever, I am seeing flower
Asking her,
From you, forever

Tonight come, take dark the world
Your sorrow, make me taken, burn
Shinn my sparkling gold

I hate to be as sleep's swamp
As the whale, love the deep seas
You are my Ocean, let me swim
Up my sun, hot me

When I see your hair, as the tempting waves
Always Juicy, Like a Cypress
Wonderful, tear drop in your eyes gray

Make emotion of drunk
So shine as wine in Rhine

Please, fly to me in moon light
GIRL:
Answer to me in cute:
"When I have goes to you, my love
No need to light"

14- Let's be better

This messiah bright morning,
As the baby of novelty, smile
This clear heaven morning,
The mirror of God, is sign

Like turquoise, her bright spire
As if march sky
That face is washed, seen in distant,
It is obvious glory of mountain

The manor comes from the breeze to the flower
Similar to mother and son's love
What the nature's Warp, are blest for this song

Alas, as the sun rises
No longer is that pleasant pleasure
No longer is this sweet smile
No longer is this delight

It's a day and ravage of cheaters
In the area of fraud and trick
Day and the outcry hypocritical
Called "human destruction", is theatrical!

Again, How to loot!
How much cost human blood?

There is a lot of deception instead faith
There is a lot of lies instead swear
Primitives were not like this
No, no, these are not the same

Till night is so common
Tomorrow is the same routine

Oh, that beautiful dawn, so shine,
What is the bond with this dark sunset?
Days pass on us
But that's so annoying for wise

In my biography if you want to know
More than a hundred years
Lived in cities with people
Bite the bullet, day and night

Finally, I asked the desert
To anyone,
I would like to go somewhere since man
No reminders, no faces, no name

One desperate, in those burning wild land
Sleeping on the ground
My endless grief,
Talked with a camel, scorpion or wind
Singing, I was singing;
Desert by desert, I am going free, free
No longer hear of human being

In those deserts confide my life
Give up and Hold at the paw of fiery sun
Be safe from sword shadow of the arch

Certainly, if it was possible of inhumanity flight,
  Like the town, desert become full of mankind

Whoever you are, look yourself sometimes
Good job, but be better than you are!

15- Last Floor, moon

Last Floor, coffee please, 20+1 Room
What a pleasure, drinking coffee on the top floor!

Watching the city with several billion lights on
Cars like worker ants
Sub heads carry on the way
Such as bison herd
All together brakes
Red dots in nested paths

In that high,
Everything is very small
Statue of Liberty more like a toy
I am a higher than all
Even that my vile boss,
As proud as pea cock
As bald as a coot

Simply, I grow up
Several times a day
I am higher to another
Thank you elevators
Simply, coming me up
I want to stay in this room above all

Then, everyone who wants show me,
With fingers point to the sky!

What exciting news:
I tickle the moon with finger
No reason to fear

16- JEALOUS

All in my world is your joy
All of my concern is your little woes
All I need is meet your needs
Your migraine even fake,
Cause the death of me

Unduly your smiles, reason to my life
Aware! You are my wizard Orb
In you, I would forget who I am?
In out, I would forget to breathe, furthermore,
Oxygen which I want for you

When you're not with me
There is so much air
But I have no reason to breathe

I can't imagine just a moment, parted to you
Even in sleep I can't tolerance,
You are gone alone in other place
Yeah I am **Jealous**
Just I'm pounding in your chest

My hobby is drinking in your cup that is grate
Take my waist in dance, keep pace
I won't see your lips red by wine, serious
Told you before: I am **Jealous**

I feel sound of your walk
You say me Hi and I …
Make me a Falter
So disturbed inside of me
Spark!
Instead reply
Forgive my heart

Thrown in the river of life the fishing hooks
I caught you, lovely
 You can't pull, can you?

My eyes taking photo from you with 100 M.P
Resolution
In my heart I publish hundred times
Then divided between my cells
Now, I'm art gallery in your mind

17- Imaginary east

Sun takes a head into out of the window, in cute
To the east imagination,
You,
More bright morning
Head on my side
With face as the rose's bloom
Smile!!!

I,
More clean sun
See,
In your kindly smile
In Exciting flourish rise

Todays, I
With the sun of your face
Rising on my Fantasy orient
Begin

I am writing for you
Sing with you
Talk to you,
 With you walk
Oh, from the passion of this fantasy to,
Your hand in my hand
Instead walking

I would fly

That time, shocked
In my isolation or
Between others
Sit silent…
I hear your eyes song

Sometimes between others, in the busy town
Except your face, I forget all

Unaware People say to together, light:
Here, here…See the crazy!
Random like babies, laugh
With himself, how he talk?
I take no care on usually blame
Still dead drunk
In the Space of mysterious
Upbeat for my fate
How do I talk: Wise!
I'm not fool,
 In God
Intensity "I am in love"

18- I swear to woman

In this world without woman, no fondness, no kindness
When the heart of died, be dead psyche
No wrote in any liber, fate;
Lack for women, for men perfect

I swear to you, I swear

The first base of universe, they were
Who has building a house without foundation?
If a woman not be alight, as candle
Nobody see end of direction

In the born time, she was like an angel
Devils were teased her
If Plato and Socrates were great
Because her mother had fostered them

I swear to you, I swear

If hero, if seeker, if scholar or the pious
All of them are mother's school pupil
If women no darn dress of man
Men's cloths was rag

Friend and compassionate, in the health date
Patron and ally, in incident day

Since the opening wisdom school, they are not stupid
When the art is shin, were they hide's? "As if"

Woman, who is beloved masterpiece
From the God's masterpieces
Inspiring the minds of lover
In the role of the artist

Amplifier for soul, in love speaking
World thanks her laugh
In novelty as the hope morning
Like breathing in Andes hillside
God look to woman well, see;
Her roles in creation, a lot worthy
God your friend, ever
Do not fall into the trap of devil

I swear to you, I swear

Your essence is truthful
The magic and trick, Let lose

19- Shadow in the night

Although always city night,
With clouds and breath fumes
Dark, foggy and cold
Shadows were stolen and destroyed

I with a charm which my wizard taught me
Hide from his eyes, my shadow
Going around in foggy town,
Together,
Here, there, up and down

Anywhere he came that I was told
In the alleys of the old
Busy pub full of bulk uproar
Muslims, Christians, turkey
With a low ceiling, Lights lost in smoke
He saw also me
The pair who together slowly,
To chatter, laughter with power in their eyes, so,
Aging and death in their grim dens
Make them disappointed, fine

Shadow demanded wine
He poured, I drunk
I poured, he drunk
Lost in the island

We were in the empty rich time!

We saw and heard,
Cups that meet together
And dizzy eyes and hands
It's crazy drunk who sings

Some body cry as a child
Another, she said:" my Friend, I am afraid of nothing"
Unless, I am in love!

With frequent grail
I got drunk as my shadow
Along with elusive trice
Came back to alleys

By my Shadow, too drunk
We are drunk, drunk, drunk
Drunk and so will be trust

Oh shadow as I on the ground
Arise, is midnight, get up
No hand, no wall
No leg, no walk
Without you, no sign of me
Stay with me a unique nice
Stand up,
Without you, I am lost
Talk to me my legendary quiet!
Please, I wish know!
Reply to me, dear shadow!

Which star suddenly do sunset?
That dark's depth is too long term

20- Fly

My sweetheart, Call me
To my night grief over
Call, because the end of the time
Set my mind to you

Call me, because I believe in your meet
Behind the cloud,
The moon is found

Your voice
From behind the door
Do you remember the first meeting day?

Even, Your sounds
From distant lands
Bring me up to the mirth kingdom

Call me such as light ray
Make alive, all my cells

Over my shoulder, flew to the far plains
And then …
You can't find what occurred on me!

You was jump but,
Where is your nest?

I don't know about land of nostalgia,
Show me, where?

Oh swallowtail your wings to sky
Killed me departure
Fly, fly and fly

21- Fireplace

I wake up as an arouse
Raining
I blow
The air is close
House is desolate
Ah …
Heaven forbid you're gone

I don't eat breakfast by the window more
No newspapers,
Watching TV, no
No call by phone, no
I can't live in a house that you're not

I have anything to do with you
Just beside me,
Turn my mind to you
This is the fireplace that you,
You have the turn on, pale blue
And I, along with
To hope Fire wood
To re-coming, you

I could not to do anything, but
Said to the photographer
Take a picture from your last lough

Today, I want rain,
Since,
I have an excuse,
To ones again,
Follow you with umbel

Day without sun
Rain without Tent
Start without end
Night without moon
I without you
Odious anything itself without its complementary

Clue of my kiss
Do not clean out on your cheeks
Because, it is my mark
To the people, I ask

Standing by rely on your absence days
Strong and reliable on way
To hope that the moment of your coming
Then destroyed in your arms

Laugh means for I;
Hope for the coming
Still, windows is open wide
Alley has been jolly by your smell
House has been filled on your air
I do not believe lose you, never
Fireplace has been afire, again

22- Everest is unrest

Oh, white giant of the captive
Colum of the wide sky, oh, Everest
The steel helmet on your head
Of iron on between, have one belt
To human's eyes no see your face
Hide in clouds,
Your faces beloved

As the land was of oppression days,
Cold, dark, revolving and silent
Knock fists of fury on go-round
That fist you are; Everest Mountain

You are coarse fist of times
Relics from centuries
Ah land fist, up to the sky
Drive fists of pain on mankind
No, no you're not fist the time
Mountain! No pleased to this talk
You are ground's depressed heart
Of pain has swelling, in upon a time

You can Explode, ah, the earth's heart
Do not let's fire be hidden inside of you
Do not turn off! Talk
Brave good Laugh!

I open your mouthpiece
Even if slash all my meat
Will send out of my Heart, arc
Your flame which fears all sharks

Be freedom and Shout
Like the monster free from the chain
Your voice create the earthquake
From north to south, east to west
The power of your stokehole, shine
From deep to high

Make a unique combine
Make unique mixture
Gas, fire, and brimstone
Rock, stench and Smoke
From the anger of innocent mankind
And the flame of God's punishment

Clouds send to us
Rain of fear, offense and shock
Just like in "Ad" or in Pompeii
Vulcans pour suspended death

Destroy foundation of hypocrisy
Fall to pieces this breed and bond
Dig root of this evil build which must
By root burned this black, this dark

23- End of probability theory

We live in an age of Probability
In an age of skepticism
In the time of weather forecast

From each side of the wind comes
Everybody suspect to uncertainty;
New times

An era which nothing in it,
In the certain probability
But, I
Without, your name
I had no existence certainly, even second

Your eyes,
You look firmly, my religion
Paint of your name,
Written on the wings of angel
Mirrors,
By reflecting of your name, laugh
Your name, all the caveman,
Once upon a time
Wrote on the rocks

Between sleep and wakefulness
I sit front of you, right now; at the moment boundless

Is it still can once again?
Go high excited, up to the stairs!

Best Moments
Moments in our novel
Tales from any time& anywhere
Story is love story
Wonderful, meet with you, really!
The end of probability theory

My life,
Empty of mid people &half
The one person is
All, pure, full time love

The night's mystery to "Wallflower" I asked
They certainly know this right
Since their essence,
Always in the night, spread
Such a romantic, they said: You are

24- Dogs & Wolfs

It is cold, snowing is heavy
Silent cloud and gray,
For the land shekel, shekel,
Sends cover a very bulky

The song of night hut without holes
Song of rain and snow
The howling of wind is awareness!
' Hurricane is guest of tonight, whole

Runner on scene of snow, wind
Flowing on the wings of wind, sting
Stormy night, blizzard,

"Singing dogs":
The land is cold, wet, infected
It is dark with angry gale
Wind screams like wolves, howler
But we are lucky, what is the fear?
Near the treasury of the Lord, there;
So soft sleep on the mattress
What is enjoyable and then;
He says oh my dear; come here

Take leftover from the king
And it's not, some of the bones!

What a beautiful life, fair wind!
What a kindness dear Lord

Have you hear about it? Yes, lash
"Face the music", we have to pass

Although it is true that is painful
But Lord's mercy, we have to wait
Because his anger will fall
He lets put my head on his shoes, his feet
Count our wounds,
 We thanks this love

"Singing wolfs"
The land is cold, wet, infected
It is angry gale and dark
Wind screams like dogs, bark
Full attack, earth is join in sky
Wild night and grisly storm,
Rule on the plains and us,
No hot niche corner,
Mountain slots or shelter

Not even a small grove that can,
For relax sometimes with unstressed

Two enemies ambush to us, constant
Two enemy, tortured us
Outside cold monster, inside the hungry dragon;
To gripe on our organs

And now, the third enemy, snap
Come outside the den and attack

Firearms and cruel
Between deep blue sea and the devil

Drink up snow! Be rosy, up blaze
This blood is ours, for homeless
For hungry wolves!
Blood of sons of wilderness

Our tribe,
In this cold; hungry, wounded
Running on the snow anxiously, as wind
But dignity of freedom;
Preserve strongly, "we are free"!

25- Dangerous

Be an unidentified man, Pleas!
One new persons is dangerous
Don't look at me, no beside me, be loss
Intense distress is serious

I am as the end days of December
The end of the calendar is perilous
How many escape routes in your heart, may?
The Locks in the night,
Without key
Is disastrous

I am not comfort, my number is up
No speck of hope! The vampire in top, is murderous
Your world is hell, even your Godly
"Faith to me" too, is hazardous.

Your feed was my blood, no more
But you can't rob my soul,
It is forever, you know!

26- Concept of love

Your remember in my mind, forever, it is right
Hey, without you, my eyes, Fountain of tears night
Hey, When You Went Away
From east of my lips, laughs Sunrise gone
It was a sign of storm

Oh, When You went
Moonlight in roof sky, was paler
Universe in my eyes ... was more tightened than cage
Yeah, the prisoner of waves

By and by,
The leaf were yellow, sun depression
Hey, When You Went Away
Death laughed
Died sense to live in my heart

From the Wind asked, do you see?
Said: that I sought lost…
Blow, all of the world
Grief, Grief
Can't see, brief

I ask to night
She said: Alas, alas

I stayed dark! For months,
To await her rise

To thunder, asked from your name
His voice echoed in the dome heavens
As the bereaved mothers, wail

I told your eyes story to cloud
She was crying on the ground ... in sorrow
Without meaning, tomorrow

27- ALBERT iron his socks

My behavior is normal

But I do not know why?
These days,
From family and friends
Everyone see me
From afar say:
"Seems, these days,
You are at the see"

But, I am as every day
With the simple Address
And with the same sign
The same normal action
As always, quiet

These days, only
I feel sometimes a little ambiguous
Sometimes a little confused

I feel some days before,
I love these days, much more

I sing with rocks
And grateful to moments, so good
These days, sometimes
From the days, month, the calendar
Of newspapers, I am unaware
Sometimes I feel a little less
Sometimes, highly best
Even if I would talk
In different way, I worship God

Last night, again
Than the other night was so cruel
I was completely shut down

I sat down good
I iron my socks
I walked in my room, only seven miles!
I talk with my shoes,
Then all letter, up and down
Between all the row,
Followed by a fictitious legend
I was looking for the unknown
Saw nothing
But wait!
I feel a weird smell from one of them!

Last night, again
I was swing among the galaxy clusters, eager
Went up clouds ladder, in space

I spin in the sky
And my pocket,
Filled cloud patches

I wish you were there
A mouthful crisp of milk way
A piece of the moon,
I ate

Newly these days, I realized
I love the red rose more than white
To remember for small moments
I would celebrate four days

Rest assured,
Beyond these feelings that I said
I do not have another mood
My feet are quite naked

Albert Einstein didn't like wearing sock*

28- A seat next to President!

She drives me crazy, my roof with over thousand channels
For some times, may be now,
Channel seven plays my show

I am involved
 Every night for 45 minutes
Since I was no born,
I see to the next three years, oh!

I don't like,
The last part
I don't want,
To die!
It is brutal!

I bought an expensive car, Last night
Bringing money by truck in car store, dump
 Quite smart!
I had ticket to Paris, by a famous airline,
Tonight
My seat Booked next to the president!

If you know what's scary!
That parts fall in love, get married
I wish Censored or pass speed
May I am pretending to sleep?
When my father went from here forever, I was fifteenth
 I did not see my mother again, from Sixteenth

Query I realized, she died;
That women was playing my mother role
No one can play her figure

Even though serial is bitter, I love it, at no cost
Even, I do not turn it off,
After my mind's eye sleep, it will be shut down
There's only one problem: no replay!
I decide after season fine
With little change, start story again!